I0813164

DISCOVERING THE UNITED STATES

Wisconsin

BY MARY SHAW

Kids Core
An Imprint of Abdo Publishing
abdobooks.com

abdobooks.com

Printed in China.
052024
092024

Cover Photo: Shutterstock Images
Interior Photos: Tony Tomsic/AP Images, 4–5; Bettmann/Getty Images, 6; Jim Schwabel/Shutterstock Images, 7; Jukka Jantunen/Shutterstock Images, 9 (top left); iStockphoto, 9 (top right), 14; Shutterstock Images, 9 (bottom left), 12–13, 18, 25, 26, 28 (top left); Gerald Corsi/iStockphoto, 9 (bottom right); Bruce Bennett/Getty Images Sport/Getty Images, 10; Louis Lopez/Cal Sport Media/Alamy Live News/Alamy, 16; Sean Pavone/Shutterstock Images, 20–21; Nejdet Duzen/Shutterstock Images, 23; Red Line Editorial, 28 (top right), 29; Jacob Boomsma/Shutterstock Images, 28 (bottom left); Rudy Balasko/Shutterstock Images, 28 (bottom right)

Editor: Marley Richmond
Series Designer: Katharine Hale

Library of Congress Control Number: 2023949380

Publisher's Cataloging-in-Publication Data

Names: Shaw, Mary, author.
Title: Wisconsin / by Mary Shaw
Description: Minneapolis, Minnesota: Abdo Publishing, 2025 | Series: Discovering the United States | Includes online resources and index.
Identifiers: ISBN 9781098294212 (lib. bdg.) | ISBN 9798384913481 (ebook)
Subjects: LCSH: U.S. states--Juvenile literature. | Wisconsin--History--Juvenile literature. | Midwest States--Juvenile literature. | Physical geography--United States--Juvenile literature.
Classification: DDC 973--dc23

All population data taken from:
"Estimates of Population by Sex, Race, and Hispanic Origin: April 1, 2020 to July 1, 2022." *US Census Bureau, Population Division*, June 2023, census.gov.

CONTENTS

Vince Lombardi coached the Packers from 1959 to 1968. The team won many championships during this time.

CHAPTER 1

Go Pack Go!

It was December 31, 1967. The Green Bay Packers were hosting the National Football League (NFL) Championship. The game was at Lambeau Field in Green Bay, Wisconsin. The temperature was −18 degrees Fahrenheit (−28°C).

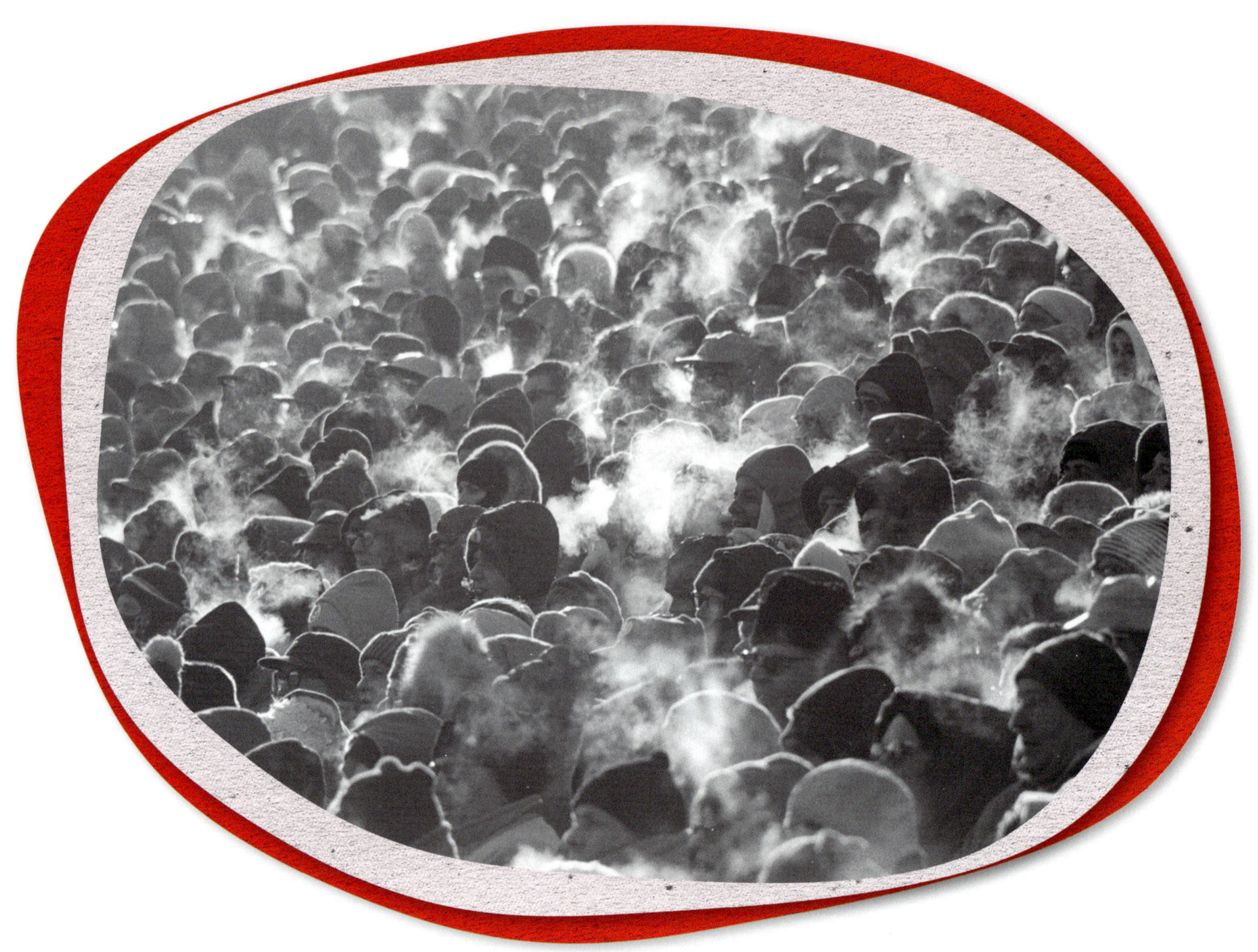

Despite the cold, more than 50,000 fans watched the Packers play on December 31, 1967.

Football fans braved the cold to fill the stands. The Packers were losing 17–14 to the Dallas Cowboys. There were only 16 seconds left in the game. Then, Packers quarterback Bart Starr scored a touchdown. The Packers

Wisconsin has more than 800 miles (1,290 km) of shoreline along Lake Superior and Lake Michigan.

had won! This was the third time in a row Wisconsin had won an NFL Championship.

Wisconsin's Land

Wisconsin is in the Midwest region of the United States. The state borders Michigan and Lake Superior to the north. To the east is Lake Michigan, and to the south is Illinois. Minnesota and Iowa are to the west.

The Wisconsin River crosses the state from north to south. The Mississippi River runs along the western border of Wisconsin. Bald eagles live near these water sources to catch fish.

Parts of Wisconsin used to be covered in **glaciers**. These glaciers had fully melted by about 11,000 years ago. They left behind lakes

On the Ice Age Trail

On the Ice Age Trail, hikers can see land features that were left behind by melting glaciers. These glaciers began to melt about 16,000 years ago. Before then, animals such as woolly mammoths roamed the land. The trail's logo shows a woolly mammoth. The trail stretches nearly 1,200 miles (1,930 km).

Wisconsin Facts

DATE OF STATEHOOD
May 29, 1848

CAPITAL
Madison

POPULATION
5,892,539

AREA
65,496 square miles (169,634 sq km)

STATE BIRD

American robin

STATE TREE

Sugar maple

STATE FLOWER

Wood violet

STATE ANIMAL

Badger

Each US state has a different population, size, and capital city. States also have state symbols.

and hills that are still around today. **Bluffs**, plains, and marshes also make up Wisconsin's landscape. Animals such as elk and deer live in the state's forests.

Some Wisconsinites take advantage of freezing temperatures by playing ice hockey on frozen lakes.

Wisconsin's Climate

Wisconsin's climate varies depending on the season. Summers are hot and can be **humid**. Leaves begin to change color in the fall when the weather gets cooler.

Freezing temperatures and heavy snowfall are common in Wisconsin during winter. The snow begins to melt in spring. But surprise snowfalls have happened as late as May.

Explore Online

Visit the website below. Does it give any new information about the history of the Green Bay Packers that wasn't in Chapter One?

Green Bay Packers

abdocorelibrary.com/discovering-wisconsin

Members of the Ho-Chunk Nation perform traditional songs and dances.

The People of Wisconsin

American Indians have lived on the land that is now Wisconsin for at least 10,000 years. Peoples such as the Ho-Chunk, Potawatomi, and Ojibwe have lived in the region since the 1600s. Many American Indian people in Wisconsin ate wild rice.

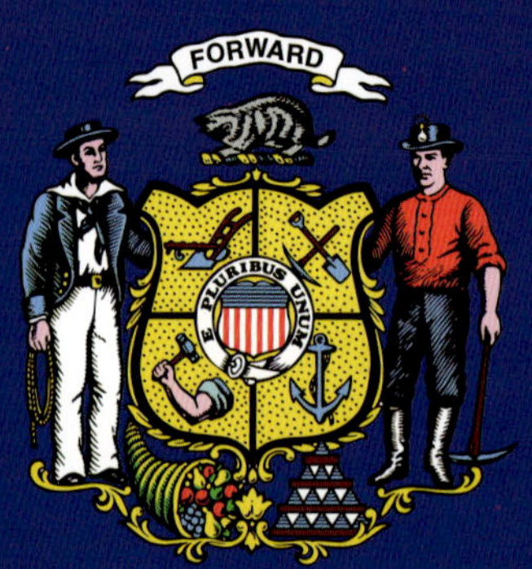

The Wisconsin flag shows the state's motto, "Forward." This motto represents progress.

They made maple sugar from maple trees. These foods are still important parts of many American Indian cultures. Today Wisconsin has 11 federally recognized American Indian nations.

Europeans began **immigrating** to Wisconsin in the early 1800s. Many Germans came to the state. They were followed by

Norwegian, Swedish, and Polish settlers. Hmong **refugees** began arriving in the 1970s.

Nearly 5.9 million people live in Wisconsin today. The state's population is about 80 percent white and 7 percent Black. More than 3 percent of Wisconsinites are Asian, and 1 percent are American Indian. About 8 percent of the population is Hispanic or Latino.

Many famous people have called Wisconsin home. Writer Laura Ingalls Wilder was born in the state. Wilder's most famous book is *Little House on the Prairie.*

Wisconsin Culture

Football is a big part of Wisconsin's culture. Packers fans are called Cheeseheads.

On game days, many Packers fans wear the team colors of dark green and gold. Some people wear Cheesehead hats.

The Green Bay Packers' home stadium is Lambeau Field. Home games are very popular. Many fans gather to watch games together.

Thanks to Polish immigrants, polka is Wisconsin's state dance. During the fourth quarter of Packers games, the stadium plays a polka song. Football traditions are also inspired by German immigrants. Brats served with **sauerkraut** are a popular dish at football games.

Many Wisconsinites also like to explore the great outdoors. The cold doesn't stop people from enjoying time outside. Ice fishing on frozen lakes is a common winter activity.

Major Industries

Wisconsin's nickname is America's Dairyland. The state is the top US producer of cheese.

The Lumberjack Games

The Lumberjack World Championships are held in Hayward, Wisconsin, each summer. Events include log rolling, axe throwing, and speed pole climbing. Some participants can climb 90 feet (27 m) in less than one minute!

More than 3 million cows live on farms in Wisconsin.

Wisconsin has rich soil that is good for raising animals and growing crops. Many farmers grow soybeans, cranberries, and potatoes.

Many Wisconsinites work in **manufacturing**. The Milwaukee Electric Tool Company is a major employer. Tourism is another important industry in Wisconsin. Millions of people visit the state every year.

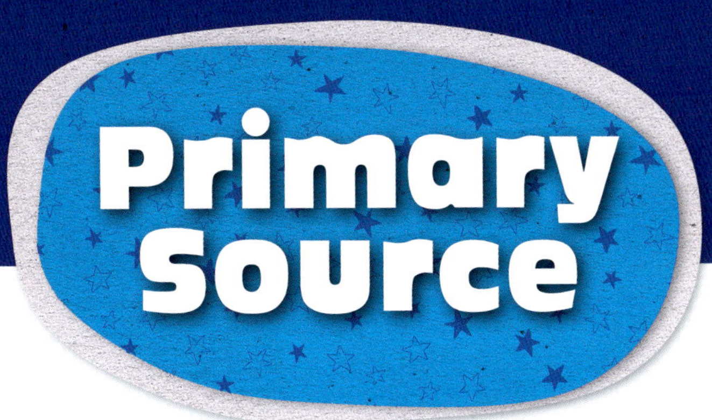

Latricia, a Hmong farmer, has been growing vegetables in her family's garden for years. She and her family grow foods to make traditional meals. She shares her harvest with other Hmong refugees. Latricia said:

> It's nice to have fresh food on the table . . .
>
> and to continue the traditions of our culture.

Source: "A Heartland Holiday Feast: The Hmong in Rural Wisconsin." *PBS*, n.d., pbs.org. Accessed 9 Nov. 2023.

Point of View

What is the author's point of view on this topic? What is your point of view? Write a short essay about how they are similar or different.

Milwaukee is on the shore of Lake Michigan.

CHAPTER 3

Places in Wisconsin

Wisconsin's largest city is Milwaukee. Milwaukee has many museums to visit, including the Milwaukee Art Museum. Madison is Wisconsin's capital. People can visit the Olbrich Botanical Gardens there. Olbrich has indoor and outdoor gardens.

Eau Claire hosts music festivals such as the annual Eau Claire Jazz Festival.

The Great Outdoors

There are many places to explore the outdoors in Wisconsin. The Apostle Islands is a National Lakeshore. Visitors can take boats out to visit these islands on Lake Superior.

Door County is on a **peninsula** surrounded by Lake Michigan. It is famous for its cherry trees

The Apostle Islands

There are 21 different Apostle Islands. Many have sea caves to explore. Kayakers can paddle from island to island. They can also visit beaches and lighthouses. Scuba divers can swim around shipwrecks in Lake Superior.

People often visit Door County in the fall to see the colorful autumn leaves.

and nature. The Saint Croix National Scenic Riverway borders Minnesota. People can kayak down the Saint Croix and Namekagon Rivers.

Wisconsin has many state parks. Big Bay State Park is on the edge of Madeline Island on Lake Superior. It is far from city lights, so it is the perfect place for stargazing. Many parks are open year-round. Cross-country skiing is a popular winter activity.

Devil's Lake State Park is in Baraboo. People can see effigy mounds there. These are ancient and sacred mounds of earth made by Ho-Chunk people.

Landmarks

Lambeau Field isn't the only popular football destination in Wisconsin. The Wisconsin Badgers are the University of Wisconsin–Madison's team. The Badgers play at Camp Randall Stadium.

People can hike through Devil's Lake State Park to see rock formations. One formation is called Devil's Doorway.

The House on the Rock is another unique place to visit in the state. The attraction has themed rooms and exhibits. Visitors can explore a circus room, a dollhouse room, and many more.

More than 4 million people visit the Wisconsin Dells each year.

Wisconsin Dells is famous for its attractions. Noah's Ark Waterpark is a popular destination. Mount Olympus Resort has a large amusement park with many wooden roller coasters.

Wisconsin's culture and history can be seen in the food, dance, and traditions of the state. People can enjoy Wisconsin any time of year. Whether going ice fishing or watching a football game, there is always something fun to do in Wisconsin.

Further Evidence

Visit the website below to see photos of the Apostle Islands. Does it give any new evidence to support Chapter Three?

Apostle Islands

abdocorelibrary.com/discovering-wisconsin

State Map

KEY

City or town

Point of interest

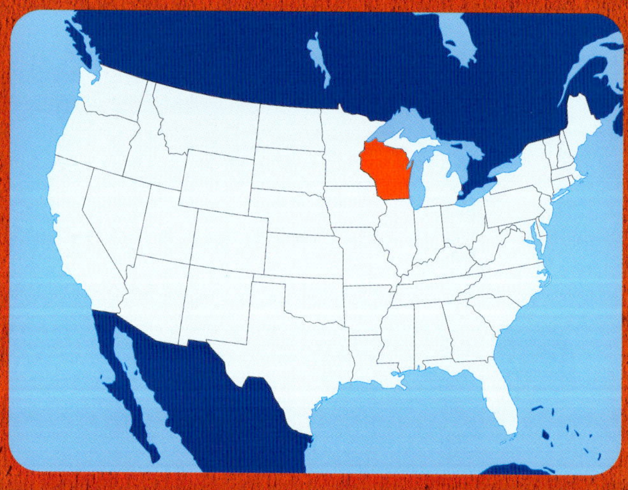

La Crosse

Madison

Wisconsin: The Badger State
Apostle Islands
Lake Superior
Big Bay
State Park
Michigan
Wisconsin River
Door County
Eau Claire
Wausau
Lambeau
Field
Green Bay
Mississippi River
La Crosse
Minnesota
Wisconsin
Dells
Lake
Michigan
Devil's Lake
State Park
Iowa
Milwaukee
The House
on the Rock
Madison
N
W
E
S
Illinois

Glossary

bluffs
steep hills, cliffs, or banks

glaciers
masses of ice that move slowly over land

humid
describing air that has a lot of moisture

immigrating
moving to another country

manufacturing
the process of making goods to sell

peninsula
an area of land surrounded by water on three sides

refugees
people who leave a country to escape danger

sauerkraut
a dish made of fermented cabbage

Online Resources

To learn more about Wisconsin, visit our free resource websites below.

Visit **abdocorelibrary.com** or scan this QR code for free Common Core resources for teachers and students, including vetted activities, multimedia, and booklinks, for deeper subject comprehension.

Visit **abdobooklinks.com** or scan this QR code for free additional online weblinks for further learning. These links are routinely monitored and updated to provide the most current information available.

Learn More

Hunter, Tony. *Green Bay Packers.* Abdo, 2020.

Kavon, Kana. *The 50 States.* DK, 2021.

Tieck, Sarah. *Wisconsin.* Abdo, 2020.

Index

About the Author

Mary Shaw is an editor, designer, and writer of children's books. She formerly lived in Eau Claire, Wisconsin.